THE TEENAGE WORRIER'S
POCKET GUIDE TO ROMANCE

THE TEENAGE WORRIER'S

POCKET GUIDE TO

ROMANCE

Ros Asquith

as Letty Chubb

CORGI

THE TEENAGE WORRIER'S POCKET GUIDE TO ROMANCE
A CORGI BOOK : 0 552 146420

First publication in Great Britain

PRINTING HISTORY
Corgi edition published 1998

Copyright © Ros Asquith, 1998

Set in 11½pt Linotype Garamond by
Phoenix Typesetting Ilkley, West Yorkshire

Corgi Books are published by Transworld Publishers Ltd,
61–63 Uxbridge Road, Ealing, London W5 5SA,
in Australia by Transworld Publishers (Australia) Pty. Ltd,
15–25 Helles Avenue, Moorebank, NSW 2170,
and in New Zealand by Transworld Publishers (NZ) Ltd,
3 William Pickering Drive, Albany, Auckland.

The Random House Group Limited supports The Forest Stewardship
Council® (FSC®), the leading international forest-certification organisation.
Our books carrying the FSC label are printed on FSC®-certified paper.
FSC is the only forest-certification scheme supported by the leading
environmental organisations, including Greenpeace. Our
paper procurement policy can be found at
www.randomhouse.co.uk/environment

Printed and bound in Great Britain by Clays Ltd, St Ives plc

CONTENTS

ADONIS, attraction, BOYZ
Breaking-up, Chatting up,
CLUBS, CONTRACEPTION,
Double Dates, Fudge, GAYS,
GURLZ, Holiday Romances,
INFATUATION, JEALOUSY
KISSING, Love letters,
Marriage, NAUGHTY BITS,
Orgasm, Poetry, PREGNANCY,
Questions? RED ROSES SEX,
Seasons, TELEPHONE, TRUST
VALENTINES,
UNDERWEAR, VIRGINS, WATER, xcitement
YES, zits – and More

Heart-shaped pillow
Waterbed
Luxury Suite
ROMANTIC Wayside Inn
Lurvers' Lane
Remotesville
Isle of View
Hotsex
KISS
1LUV U2

Dearest Teenage Worrier(s),

   Is there a certain someone who makes your heart race like drum'n'bass, your legs feel bendier than silly string, your face feel as if each cheek had turned into a grilled tomato? Do you weep deep into the night? Gaze for hours at a time at blurry photo? Keep fragments of lurved one's old chewing-gum under tear-stained duvet?
   Here, at long last, is the handy Pocket Guide that brings you all the secrets of True ROMANCE: how to find the perfect partner; how to trap them in a willy (sorry, wily) NET; how to KEEP them there by stunning ruses such as, um, knowing how to stimulate their vital zones (phew, hurl self into ice bucket) and how to be V.V.V. Interesting while remaining elusively Kooool Etck.
   I shall also be showing how to avoid all those tragic ROMANTIC worries that plague the life of the average spotty, greasy, pudding or beanpole-shaped Teenage

1

Worrier of the twenty-first century.

Such as: MUST I really go out with someone when I am V. Happy by myself? HAS everyone else on planet had sex except moi? WHEN that V.V. Attractive, dazzling, witty, intelligent person ignores me as though I were a mere ant, does it really mean they lurve me but are too kool to show it? OR is it they just don't care for the name 'Ant', arf arf, argh Etck. (NB Quick answers to the above questions are no, no and um (sorry), no.

*It will tell you all about **Dates**: How to get one; How to avoid one; How to look; What to do . . . How Not to Care too much. How to say get lost, get found Etck.*

As my fan(s) will know, I haven't quite solved all of these myriad lurve-worries moiself just yet, but in the process of writing this advice-packed tome, I am sure I will advance to greater self-knowledge and enhance my ability to entrap any passing male that takes my fancy. I feel V.V. Highly qualified to talk of such matters now, as I have actually KISSED three whole boyz (well, akshully, only bits of their faces of course, ahem). I think this is a V. High number for someone of my humble age (although if you listened to some of the liars at my skule you wd think they had Done It with everyone in Universe) although I must admit that in each case I have only kissed them once, so I that I have still not, um, Gone the Whole Way, nor am I likely to until I am well over the age of consent, due to:

1) Lack of opportunity
2) Fear of breaking law

2

3) *Fear of catching terminal illness*
4) *Fear of not knowing what bit to put where (will this buke help?)*
5) *Lack of interest (not mine, the boyz; they are always looking over my shoulder at my frend Hazel)*

ROMANCE, anyway, is different to sex. It is about longing, dreaming, hoping, wanting, yearning, swooning, lusting, slavering, snogging (whoops, phew, ice bucket again).

So put away that box of tissues, close your ears to the screech of violins and the wail of banshees that make the life of a Teenage-Worrier-in-Lurve so tragic and learn how to, um, think positive (wish I could) and look on Bright Side (bright side of what?). In short, I will expose all the daft advice other bukes land you with and hope that by the time you've got from A to Z, you will either get happy in ROMANCE or throw this buke at the moron who doesn't care about you.

And go on to better boyz. Or gurlz.

—Lurve, as ever,

Letty Chubb

X X

An INTRO TO MOI . . .

A few werds about the ROMANCES of my life so far, full details of which you can find soulfully relayed in my three previous tomes . . .

Brian 'Brain' Bolt

Not exactly right for ROMANCE category, as although Brian faithfully cleaves to *moi*, I would really prefer to spend the day with my little brother's gerbil, Horace, who, come to think of it rather resembles Brian but lives much more exciting life. If a three-metre-high Valentine card arrives on Feb *13th* in order to embarrass the householder and give the recipient a day in which to return the favour, it will have Brian's exquisite copperplate hand upon it. But it is not his spots, or his fluffy teeth, that put me off Brian. It is more his obsessive, doggy devotion to *moi*. And, of course, that incident with the bicycle wheel and the flour . . .

Daniel Hope

The first true lurve of my LIFE, Daniel Hope still has hair the colour of wet sand at sunset (I tried to make *moi*self think it was more the colour of elastic bands when he left me but – sob – I just couldn't

4

convince *moi*self) and eyes bluer than forget-me-nots. Nonetheless he has successfully forgotten-me-often and has raised my hopes only to cruelly dash them on the rocks of despair by abandoning me on *three* separate occasions, twice with two of my best friends. Tragickly, ROMANCE being what it is, I know that if I glimpse his manly form, or hear his sonorous tones, I am liable to swoon. On principle then, I only allow myself to pass his house (which involves, I admit, an elaborate detour from my school route) about four times a week. There is still something about being on the street where he lives . . .

Adam Stone

Daniel may be beautiful, but he has a wilful and negligent soul. Adam, whose hair is like little bunches of grapes, whose eyes are twin coals gleaming with mischief and smouldering with unleashed pashione, is as honest as the Day is Long. As noble as a knight of olde. As truthful as little Georgie Washington. And in Los Angeles. It is my tragedy that he escaped there because I was too foolish to believe his lurve for *moi* . . . Nightly I weep into my pillow (I wonder if I shld change pillowcases more often? Maybe this is why I sneeze so much) and beat my little fists against the walls in an agony of tribulation. Did he get my letter explaining All? Should I write again? I write nightly, but tear up my efforts. Oh, Adammmmmm, Adaaaaaam, is your soul like your surname? Will you never return?

With heavy pen, dear reader, I return to the task of this brief guide, hoping to inject a little hope, a little joy, into my life which is otherwise blighted by failed ROMANCE. Thank goodness I am comforted still by my only faithful lurve – my cat **Rover**. She may make me sneeze even more than my sodden pillow, but at least she is here . . .

NB If you buy loads of this book, maybe I can scrape up the fare to L.A. and see my darling Adam again, even if it is only once . . . even if it is to see him in the arms of Sharon Groan . . .

Adonis

THE BUTTERFLY of Romance FLUTTERS BY

Glorious Youth beloved of Venus, the goddess of Lurve, and therefore a term used to describe V. Fanciable blokes up to the present day. ie: that is, Daniel and Adam (swoon). However, it is V. worth bearing in mind that Brian Bolt may one day be seen as an Adonis by someone or something, possibly a relative of Benjy's gerbil. That day can't come too fast for me. The Adonis is also a pleasant species of butterfly — let no-one accuse me of failing to educate you, dear reader(s).

Attraction

Is that magnetic force that impels you towards someone, drawn by mysterious X-Files-type force Etck. It is as mysterious — and invisible — as the elemental force of gravity on all of earth's inhabitants as discovered by Isaac Newton shortly before going into coma when apple fell on head. The great thing about attraction is, everyone has got some of it. It is not about simple things like having big bazoomz Etck, but about mysterious chemical substances like pheromones, which we all give off and which some people give off more of than others. This partly explains universal oddities like: why is person who looks like the back of a car ferry always pursued by fifty panting hunks? Or hunking pants. Why is V. Beautiful person sad and lonely? Etck.

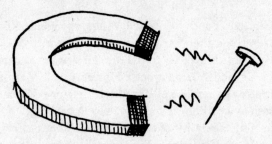

Magnets attract – but also repel. Ask yourself:
do you really <u>WANT</u> that nail? No rude remarks about
screws, <u>per-LEASE</u>).

However, not being attractive to the person you have set your heart on does not mean you have no pheromones, just that the right person for your particular brand hasn't turned up yet. Also, whether you attract people has as much to do with your own mood as how you look. And this in turn has to do with confidence. Confidence is what we Teenage Worriers need in bucketfuls but usually have only in tiny droplets . . .

But . . . dear fellow Worriers, remember that a ROMANTIC relationship cannot thrive on affection alone, nor must it ever try to survive on pity. It must contain ye elements of *sizzle*. So, however much you LIKE someone, don't bother if you don't fancy them too. It will only lead to heartache (theirs). If it's clear they don't fancy YOU, it will also only lead to heartache (yours). If you fancy them but don't much like them, also steer clear. This could lead to even bigger heartache (cue sound effects of squalling infants, tragick Teenage Worriers alone in endless docs' waiting-rooms Etck).

If only it were so easy...

Bachelors

Unmarried males. These are what unmarried females are supposed to sniff out and lure into matrimonial web of cozy nest, nuclear family, Happy-Ever-After Etck. 'Nuclear' has always seemed to me a good word to apply to Family Life, due to loud bangs, flying objects, deadly fall-out Etck, but I think it's supposed to mean going round in circles, which is what life in *La Maison Chubb* feels like most of the time.

9

Beau

My dictionary says 'Fop, dandy, ladies' man', but maybe I shld get a more recent dictionary. Personally I like the term 'Beau', and think that reintroducing it wld enhance quality of ROMANCE. It seems to say yr LURVED one is all the things you want them to be, beautiful inside and out Etck, something to be proud of, and beautiful enough to be proud of you too Etck. That's enough on Beaux, phew, thunder of massed violins Etck.

Bezonian

The opposite. This means 'Rascal, beggarly fellow'. I also hope this isn't a description of Daniel. Wince. 'Ragamuffin' was a pretty old and confusing word to Teenage Worriers and that came back as a streetword, so why not Bezonian? 'Hey, y'all F***in' bezonians in here, shuh man!' That sort of thing . .

HEY, WOW, he's BEZONIAN INNIT?

Blind Dates

Blind dates are obviously a great idea if you don't know how to meet someone any other way, and I imagine as long as you take V. good precautions, ie: don't give address to stranger Etck, meet in V. pubic (sorry, public) place and be sure to go home early on yr own Etck, that they might provide you with a few moments of fun.

There are several different ways of getting a Blind Date:

1) A dating agency where you pay through nose to feed yr details into a computer and get a 'perfect match' i.e: You say you are a size 25 when breathing in, with a low IQ and no prospects and they magically find you a heartbreakingly handsome, solvent companion looking for just such a one as you. El Chubb is unconvinced, but I have heard of one or two successes in groups of V. old people over 25.

2) Advertise. This enables you to weed out some (but not all) weirdos and usually gives you a chance to check out their appearances. If they do not include photo – hopefully, of their face – ask yourself: why? This method is also more common for old on-shelf (joke) group.

3) Best idea for Teenage Worriers is to get a frend of a frend to fix you up with someone they think you'll like.

As long as you are V. Careful (murderers, sadists Etck have been known to seek their victims through small ads), I think these methods wld be fun. After all, everyone is lonely some of the time and most of us are lonely most of the time, so there is NO SHAME.

Boyz

Must find my boy fancy dress

The fashionable idea that Boyz are aliens from another werld (or, if you are a boy, that gurlz are aliens from another planet) was first introduced to this country by *moi*, in my best-selling buke (puff, plug) *I Was a Teenage Worrier* (still available – my Mother has six copies). However, as I pointed out then and as I still believe, boyz are more like gurlz than:

a) they like to admit
b) gurlz like to admit
c) anything else around

If you don't believe (c) above, then ask yourself, if you are a gurl, the following question: am I more like a boy than say, an armadillo, or an elephant, or a piano stool?

If you are a boy, you may like to wonder: what is more like me? A gurl? Or a cardboard box?

Of course, having established the similarities, we must remind ourselves of the differences.

More gurlz (but not all) paint their nails pale green. More gurlz (but not all) wear V. silly flimsy leg covers that get torn by minute particles of grit so they have to buy another pair after ONE DAY.

More gurlz wear V. short skirts and shave their legs. Etck.

Boyz do silly things too. But one of the silliest things boyz do, in the opinion of many (though not all) gurlz, is to pay more attention to round things like footballs and wheels than to round things like us (or straight thingz with V. microscopic round bits like *moi*). In other werds, gurlz do all the nail-painting Etck to attract boys when all boyz really want to do is skulk around in sheds comparing their valve-gear.

True Equality of Ye Sexes can only come when they do stuff which pleases themselves in equal amounts. So, boyz shld get sillier about their appearances (why should a boy in make-up be assumed to be gay?) and gurlz shld get sillier about hobbies, sez L. Chubb. However, for those of you who are interested in dating boyz, here are a handful of types to watch out for:

1) Hamlet

V. Indecisive prince who lurved his Father more than his gurlfriend and ended up killing his gurlfriend's poor old innocent father instead of his wicked uncle cos he couldn't make his mind up what to do. The poor old bloke he killed said 'To Thine own self be True' (note for illiterate Worriers: this means Be True to Yourself) which seems V. Good advice to me and more useful on ROMANCE's merry-go-round than Hamlet's 'To Be or Not to Be'. Gnash, Worry.

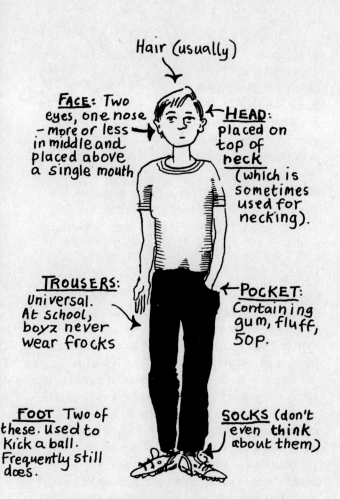

Hair (usually)

FACE: Two eyes, one nose — more or less in middle and placed above a single mouth

HEAD: placed on top of neck (which is sometimes used for necking).

TROUSERS: Universal. At school, boyz never wear frocks

POCKET: Containing gum, fluff, 50p.

FOOT Two of these. Used to kick a ball. Frequently still does.

SOCKS (don't even think about them)

Points of a <u>BOY</u> — illustrating L. Chubb's thesis that BOYZ are more like GIRLZ than anything else on Planet Earth... (so end sexist krap now) sez Chubb.

2) Boffin

This type is V.V.V.V. clever and wears specs. A boffin without specs is not a boffin, although he may be V. interllekshual. A Boffin will be more interested in the quality of light that falls on yr wig than the quality of yr wig itself and is more likely to have his mind on higher things than mare (I mean mere) emotions. Huh.

3) Shy

Gurlz are V. often attracted to V. shy boyz as they think they are deep. This is often true but is also often not. If a boy seems too shy to ask you out, it may be that he is too bored to ask you out, or the number of words necessary to do it is higher than he can count. If he is too shy to declare his everlasting lurve, ask yourself: is it possible he does not lurve me? Do not assume that shyness is the cause of his extreme lack of interest in you. If, however, you really like a shy boy, it is definitely worth trying to get him interested by asking him out, say half-a-dozen times. I would think this is as far as you can go. If this succeeds, you will still have to work V. hard to get a shy boy interested in you. Since no-one has ever shown any interest in them before, they will take a long time to believe you.

4) Sexist Pig

This is a sub-category of Yob, and though Yob behaviour almost always involves Sexist Piggery ('You've 'ad the rest, now try the best, darlin' Etck), some Sexist Pigs are cunningly disguised as non-Yobs and seem V. Interesting and Nice until you realize they expect you to always be at their beck and call, wear what they want, shut up when they're talking Etck.

Avoid this type.

5) *Perfecto*

This is the one who Has it All and Can Do It All. No point in trying to compete. Basic adulation and flattery usually work, cos the one thing they tend not to be strong on is modesty. But how can you gain their interest? Try to find one thing they're NOT good at (Needlework? Canoeing? Making model cathedrals out of matchsticks?) and devote yourself to it. This will avoid the risk of comparison in other fields and they will hopefully be convinced that you are a committed Eccentric dedicated to Yr Art.

6) *Self-Obsessed*

They say: 'We've talked enough about me, let's talk about *you* . . . What do you think of my new haircut?'

They ask for one ticket at the box office, even though you paid last time. They walk down Lurvers' Lane running their fingers tenderly through their own hair.

Avoid this type.

7) *Insecuresville*

'Oh I could never do that' they say admiringly of your teeniest accomplishments, and you are V. charmed. But they really mean it. And they are V.

Sad that they cld never do it. And they go on about how V. Sad they are that they couldn't do it. And on and on and on. V. Exhausting. If you adore an Insecuresville, your patience may be rewarded by their other sterling qualities, although personally I wld prefer to find these without the insecurities (being a V. Insecure sort of person *moi*self, worry, moan, self-doubt, despondency).

8) Beardo
(Male, usually. If a gurl with a beard, you can get it removed by electrolysis, ask yr doc.)

Some Gurlz find beards, moustaches Etck V. Romantic and arty-looking teachers with beards, or V. Caring-looking ones with beards are often the Objects of Crushes. Big bushy beards are popular with Iron John types who thrash around in forests beating their chests, howling, crying, thinking about their Mothers and trying to find their True Selves. If they find them and then have a shave they are V. Welcome to look me up, but I do not fancy kissing a bird's nest. I know it's V. Unfair that men have to shave every day, and that I have a Campaign For Hairy Armpits, Legs Etck, but personal preference only goes as far, in my case, as a soft fuzz of Designer Stubble, though even this can look V. Posey, espesh with leather coat-collar turned up. Anyway, you get the picture. All of you in LURVE with hairy Boyz can relax because they're safe from *moi*.

9) Romeo

One who everyone fancies, but who has eyes only for yoooou. Exists, possibly, but only in your dreams.

← Have censored this pic as each of us has own idea of Romeo (sigh).

Breaking up

There is an old song that says that breaking up is hard to do, and what it means is that it is hard to be left, which we all know, even if it hasn't happened to us yet. But it also means that it is hard to leave someone. Heed the advice of El Chubb: it is much better to be cruel to be kind and tell the truth *now*, rather than in two, three, or worse still thirty years' time. Never stay with someone out of pity, it just won't work. If they are trying to leave you, you have to let them do it too, instead of following first impulse, which is to plait yrself around their speeding limbs and emit long piercing howl. You definitely do not want to have six kids before he makes for the Exit, do not pass Go, do not collect gloom of spouse Etck.

TIPS FOR BREAKING UP
a) Be clear.
b) Be Kind.
c) Do not tell the person you are leaving that they are a bundle of old rubbidge. They will be feeling like that anyway.
d) Do not get back together under any circumstances for AT LEAST a year, even if you ARE lonely and tempted.
e) Remember, you broke up, so there was a REASON for it.

Hard as this is to do, always remember it is much, much worse for the person you are giving the old heave-ho to.

I often feel V. Guilty about my rejection of Brian, particularly since I inflamed his hopes Etck by going out with him again even after I'd told him it wouldn't work sharing gerbil stories with him Etck. This second episode made him miserable and, if it hadn't happened, I'd also still have a perfectly good bicycle . . .

If you are the one who is left, the best thing you can do is feel V.V.V.V. Sorry for yourself for a week. Cry constantly (preferably at a high, keening pitch), play lots of sad music and lock yourself in yr room Etck to Worry yr Mother (or other suitable caring adult) as much as possible, thereby ensuring maximum sympathy and making yourself V. Important to those around you. Over the next three weeks, emerge now and then with doleful expression to take light refreshment and allow yrself to be persuaded to sit in front of telly covered in blankets and weeping.

After one month, pick up relatively normal life. Tell yrself that Person-of-Yr-Dreams was, although perfect, Not Right For You. You cld never be happy with someone who didn't Love-you-as-you-loved-them. There is a worthier person (also better looking, funnier Etck) out there who you have yet to find. Life is worth living without a partner anyway and you are a special worthy person in yr own right Etck Etck.

Say these things to mirror every night. You will be surprised to find that within a few months you will be able to hear your lurved one's name without feeling as if you are going to die. Recovery has begun. It can only get better.

CHATTING UP

Er, sadly, the stumbling attempts of most Teen Worriers at Chatting Up will include the following touching, if naff, exchanges:

YOU: So where did you learn to do that?
HIM: What?
YOU: Hypnotize people with the back of your head. I just gazed at the back of your head for a second

and now I am hopelessly hypnotized and can think of nothing but you and will do whatever you say . . .

(NB Note bad mistake in this approach as it lays you open to total rejection. ie: he says, 'Get lost' and you have to.)

A better approach wld be:
YOU: So where did you learn to do that?
HIM: What?
YOU: Hypnotize people with the back of your head. I just gazed at the back of your head and now I feel that unless I can gaze at the front of it for the rest of my LIFE I will never be completely happy again. May I gaze at it for at least a few more minutes before you cast me into Oblivion?

(This wld take a V. hard-hearted person to refuse.)

I know it wld be V. Nice to be the recipient of such attempts to please, but you cld wait for eternity before a bloke wld summon up the courage to try these out on you, so it is better to practise yourself and not whinge if you are rejected.

CINEMA

Cinema tip: when Person-of-Yr-Dreams invites you to come to *Large Door*, do not take it at face value or as a rude remark about your size, as it will probably be the French movie *L'age D'Or* (Golden Age, to you illiterate monolingualists). This happened to me with Adam and I have since wondered whether I successfully disguised my mistake, or whether he realized at that moment that I was a true Moron.

Tip 2: do not assume that a PG, a 12 or even a U are for babies. The cinema classifications are so daft that a little bit of swearing (much less than you hear in the average household before breakfast) will shoot a film from U to 15 in milli-seconds, whereas violence quite unsuitable for one of my little brother Benjy's tender age will happily be classified PG. All you need to know before you go is: will it be so scary that I embarrass myself by hiding under seat (in the case of *moi*, this even applied to Walt Disney films until recently)? or will it be so violent I throw up into hot date's popcorn? Etck. Neither of these is advisable on a date, although a little tremor of fear can do wonders for canoodling possibilities as long as the slashing'n'burning on screen isn't too distracting.

CONTRACEPTION

This should be the Biggest Worry of all to Teenage Worriers with the slightest hope – or fear – of ever actually Doing It. But since many of you who haven't even held hands yet will think it's light years away, take El Chubb's advice: It can happen before you know it and you should be prepared. The number of single parents is rising and, arrrrg, over 70,000 are Teenagers!

Your questions answered by Auntie Letty:

I'm under 16. Can a doctor or nurse refuse to give me contraception?
They *can* but it's quite unlikely. They may suggest you talk to your parents, but they won't make you. If a doctor does refuse, go to a family planning centre. NB Remember to ask, though. They won't give you contraception if you just say you've got a sore throat and hang about looking hopeful.

But supposing they tell my family?
They won't. Doctors *have* to keep everything you tell them confidential.

Supposing my folks find out?
They'll be more likely to be happy to find a pack of
contraceptives than a little bundle of joy . . .
Anyway, they had to do stuff like this themselves
once, and were worried *their* folks might find out.
Try jogging their memories or even (gasp) talking
to them.

Won't it wreck the ROMANCE of Sex?
Not as much as a baby, or an STD (Sexually
Transmitted Disease) will . . .

*Isn't there ANY way I can get by without using
contraception?*
YES! Be a lesbian! (Gay boyz shld use condoms,
despite no fear of pregnancy). Or, stay a virgin! Or,
there's lots you can do without actually Doing It
and it is Auntie Letty's advice to experiment with
lots of fun before you actually have sex. But you
have to be careful; it's easy (so I'm told, ahem) to get
carried away, and possible, sadly, to get pregnant
without full intercourse.

So what's the best thing to use?
You've got to choose. Only two types – the female
condom and the male condom – actually protect you
against STDs (Sexually Transmitted Diseases) like
the HIV virus, which can lead to AIDS. The male
condom is a V. Effective protection and can also be
bought in supermarkets, chemists, Etck so it's worth

everyone having some of these. You also need to use them properly, which does not just mean to put them on willy rather than nose Etck, but remembering to read the leaflet thoroughly.

Other kinds include different kinds of pill (almost 100% effective in stopping pregnancy), diaphragm (sometimes called cap, but do not attempt to use on head unless being interviewed for fashion design course), implants, IUDs (devices inserted by a doctor into yr womb) and, V. recently, a male pill. Family planning centres give V. Good advice and leaflets on all of these (see details at end of buke). So, don't get drunk, have sex and THEN read a leaflet. Take Auntie Chubb's advice and BE PREPARED.

NB There is an *Emergency Contraception* you can take if you think you've slipped up. You have to take these pills within 72 hours at the latest, so ring Doc or go to clinic straight away.

DOUBLE DATING

Double dating is when four of you all go out together. It is a V. Good way of taking the heat, embarrassment, nerves, Worry, anxiety, stress, anguish, agitation (*that's enough adjectives – Ed.*) out of dating. F'rinstance, if all you can think of to say is 'what's your favourite colour?' you can just keep quiet and let three other people do the talking. Sadly, the only double date I've been on was with Hazel. This didn't work for the following reasons:

a) Both boyz spent whole evening drooling after her and ignoring *moi*.

b) She told them she was V. Sorry, but she only fancied gurlz and had only come on the date to cheer me up.

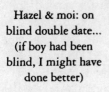

Hazel & moi: on
blind double date...
(if boy had been
blind, I might have
done better)

I wished she hadn't revealed her true nachure to them at this point as it made me feel even more plain, thick, ugly, dumb Etck. Bear this in mind if you are going on a double date and choose someone who is not most beautiful, desirable gurl in werld as your partner.

DELILAH

'Temptress, seductive and wily woman.' Sounds just like *moi* or how *moi* would be if only I had curves, bazooms Etck. But Delilah got revenge on Samson by cutting off all his wig and I would never betray Adam that way. I might feed him up a bit on V. Fattening, Pluke-Generating foods, though, so he would be less attractive to any other Delilahs he might meet. But suppose I didn't like him any more after that? Gnash, confusion, which way to go Etck?

EVE

According to ye Holey Bible, Eve was the Mother of the Human Race. Clearly, the first woman didn't have to know much about ROMANCE, since if you were the only gurl in the werld and there was only one boy, you'd be almost bound to Do It together sooner or later especially since there were not yet any magazines to read instead (or football on the telly).

And I doubt Adam (that name again – swoooooon) had to think much about flowers and chocolates, or even nuts and beetles. Contraception might have been a more useful thing for Eve to know about, since one of her sons wound up killing the other, but obviously this was one bit of knowledge she didn't get when she bit that apple.

Fetishes

Seedy adults are prone to fetishes, which are
described as abnormal (whatever that means)
stimulants to sexual desire such as, I suppose,
only being able to get an erection if you are coated
in strawberry jam and beaten with rolled-up
copies of the *Parliamentary Times*. Frankly, I am still
young enough to think such things are V.V.
UnROMANTIC and hope they are many eons away
from *moi*, but then I used to get excited at just the
brush of Adam's sleeve against mine. Phew, cold
shower.

Firsts

In ROMANCE stakes, these can roughly be honed
down to:

First Impression
That laser-beam of sexual dynamism that crosses a
room and makes your eyes pop out on stalks like in
the cartoons. Sometimes, it's followed by *an
approach*. The approach usually passes on to yr best
friend, who he asks out. You get *his* best frend, who
closely resembles a vole. However, 'vole' is an

anagram of 'love' and if this were a story, you and the vole would walk off into sunset. In real life you spurn luckless pining vole to search for another love at-first-sight type. Same thing happens all over again.

(Feb 29)

First Date
This is the one you spend five years looking forward to, five weeks building up to, five days sorting out what to wear for, five hours getting ready for, five minutes taking everything off and putting on your usual clothes for (so that you look like you haven't bothered) and five seconds on the phone when he/she rings to say they can't make it. Other scenarios include waiting outside cinema, club, bus station Etck for three hours in hailstorm refusing to believe you have been jilted. What runs through your head at such moments is: 'He must have said an hour later, silly me'. 'He forgot to put the clock forward/back two weeks ago.' 'He's been knocked down.' (And he doesn't get up again, remaining horizontal in the arms of Tania Melt).

When you finally do get to go on a date, try to be yourself. This can be difficult, if you have no idea who that is. But if you spend the whole evening being someone else, your lurved one will wonder where you have gone. Remember, if he/she doesn't like the person you at least most resemble, he/she would not have asked you out. Remember to listen to your lurved one as well as attempting to captivate

33

him/her with your dazzling wit Etck. Dazzling wit can lead to headaches. If you get that feeling that your twin souls have only been waiting for this moment to fly, tweeting and swooping, into each others' nests, this date will be likely to end with the . . .

First Kiss
Mine, as many readers will know, was with Brian Bolt, when I scratched my nose on his specs. Since then I have had a dazzling encounter with Daniel (argh! Betrayal! Revenge!) and something even better, including a fondle, from Adam. I was V. Worried about how to kiss, but I must tell you, dear reader, that although it was a disaster with Brian, it seemed to come naturally with the other two, especially – swoon, sob – with Adam. Teenage Worriers always put *How to Kiss* as a Big Worry, but, although I worried about little else for years, I was amazed how easy it was. See also KISSING.

Refusal to take the First Kiss any further (no contraceptives, do not know this person from Adam – sigh – told parents I'd be back two hours ago, V. Scared of Rising Feelings, Need Time to Think Etck) is bound to follow, as, some days later, will your . . .

First Tiff
Which, depending on how far relationship has progressed, leads to returning of letters, lurve tokens, storms of tears, recriminations Etck Etck. This is different from BREAKING UP, see earlier, as it is accompanied by much pashione: you vow never to have anything to do with each other ever again, and for two whole days you keep this promise. Since you still lurve each other, however, one of you is bound to crack, which leads to *First Reconciliation* and possibly, eventually, in far distant future when you have been canoodling for at least two years (this is a family buke) *First Actual Doing It*. Help, Worry, see SEX, CONTRACEPTION Etck.

FUDGE

No ROMANCE in the life of El Chubb is complete without juicy, subtle, crunchy, melting . . . fudge. No day is complete without fudge either, but if you wanted to woo *moi* then a bag of vanilla fudge would get you further than a bunch of roses. I mention this because

1) I hope my readers might send me any spare fudge they get, as long as not sampled first, and

2) Knowing what your lurved one really lurves is half the battle in the ROMANCE stakes.
F'rinstance, why take Sharon Sharalike to an arty French movie when she'd prefer a ringside seat at the all-women mud wrestling championship?

Gays

Are you gay? If so, you may feel alone but I promise you you are not. I've often pondered that no-one seems to be worried particularly if they fancy the opposite sex from themselves, but if they fancy the same sex they often feel rising panic, want to deny it, daren't tell their frendz, family, teachers Etck. In fact, it is just as normal to be gay as it is to be heterosexual, but less common. It is also slightly less common to have red or blond hair than brown hair but no-one thinks these things are abnormal.

The trouble with schools and other Teenage Worriers and the Big Werld Outside is that there is still a lot of prejudice out there and people still joke about gays and lesbians as though they couldn't possibly be one themselves. A lot of people are so scared of admitting they might be that they even get married and have kids before they do admit it,

Q: Which of these boyz is gay? (answer on page 68)

thus making four or five people V. Unhappy. Being Gay as a Teenage Worrier is therefore more difficult than being 'straight' (which is hard enough) and it's V. Important to be able to find other gay Teenage Worriers so you can have a good old Worry together.

Although I don't fancy gurlz myself, I sometimes have a sneaky feeling I might be happier that way, as we'd have so much more in common . . . but Hazel is still V. Shy about it and hasn't told her parents that she's a lesbian yet, which I think is a shame. As far as ROMANCE goes, the story is V. similar for gay Teenage Worriers – full of hope, lust, heartbreak Etck.

There are V. Few people who haven't ever felt a little bit ROMANTIC about someone of the same sex as themselves, so if you have these feelings just be open about them and wait and see what happens. You may fancy one, both or either sex as a Teenage Worrier and this will change as you get older, until you are sure which you prefer. Society will always push you one way, so heed El Chubb's advice and Listen to your Inner Voice. If you do what your inner voice tells you, you are much likelier to end up with Mr or Ms Right in the end.

One V. imp point is that if you have a frend who is Gay, it doesn't mean that they will fancy YOU. Lots of boyz and gurlz get worried about this, or think they may be thought gay themselves if they hang out with a Gay pal. It is very Sad to think

someone cld lose frendz this way so don't let yrself
be stoopid about it . . .

Paranoia can wreck yr life. Gay or straight,
don't make assumptions.

Grapes

Always have a bunch handy, so you can lie back with Rose between teeth (as long as Rose doesn't object, arf arf, yeech) and snarl in husky, vamp-ish tones: 'Peel me a grape.'

Gurlz

If, to gurlz, boyz are aliens from another werld then it follows that if you are a boy, gurlz are similarly from another planet. However, as I pointed out in BOYZ, earlier, gurlz are actually far more like boyz than

    a) they like to admit
    b) boyz like to admit
    c) anything else around.

Even the old idea that boyz like looking at dirty magazines Etck while gurlz just dream of ROMANCE (sigh) seems to be less true now we have unemployed gasfitters becoming strip artists Etck, and gurlz fearlessly paying to watch them show off their bits.

There is a general feeling among Teenage Worriers that gurlz are more 'mature' than boyz. But I ask you, is reading *Smirk*, or giggling over *Weenybop* any more grown-up than getting excited over *Turbo-Anorak Weekly* or *Megatit*? Is plastering your walls with pix of Brad Pitpony significantly more mature than putting up Melinda Bazoom? Is painting each finger and toenail a different pattern of silver, purple, lime green Etck any cleverer than fart-lighting?

However, one important thing that still separates the gurlz from the boyz, is that gurlz can be mothers. Being a mother also stays a BIG WISH for lots of gurlz whereas it is rare to find a boy who is longing to be a dad . . . This may make gurlz more ROMANTIC and lead them to spend time thinking how they are going to get a family.

Resist it, dear gurlz, until you are well past being a Teenage Worrier. Get a contraception and an education. Cos that prince may not come and you will have to earn a living, even if he does too. You do not want to wind up selling spotty bod on streets or dressing your five-year-old up as a baby to tempt passers-by to chuck you a few pence . . .

Hay

AAAA ACHOO?

A Roll in the hay was what Rural lurvers did. Sounds V. prickly to *moi* but preferable, as long as not highly allergic, to bike shed, urban wasteground Etck.

Holiday Romances

You are walking on tropical beach, wearing just a shimmer of polyester temptation, your hair blowing lightly against your radiant tan. Suddenly, you feel a soft burning down your back. Surely you put on your factor 2000 lotion on top of your fake-tanning-cream? You are a Worrier, after all, and do not want skin cancer. But no, the burn you feel is the searing glance of – Donatello Machismo. This dazzling stranger, a symphony of sinews complete with natty designer swimwear, mutters softly 'Are these yours?' proferring an elegant pair of, wait for it, designer sunglasses. 'N-no,' you stutter shyly, allowing your fawn-like eyes to gleam softly beneath the fronds of your newly washed, eloquently tousled mane. 'But I wouldn't mind if they were,' you add, with a look pregnant with meaning and so far little else, as he slips his golden arm round your slender waist and moves with you, as one, into the sparkling azure foam that eternally breaks against the silver sand. Ten days of bliss are followed by ten months of wondering why you never heard from him again. Surely, how could you? But surely? You gave him the wrong address? He must even now be working night and day to raise the air fare (funny, he said his dad owned a fleet of aeroplanes). And so on. You plot to return to the same place. If you are lucky enough to get there, you will be tragically confronted, on your first day, by the sight of Donatello, approaching another sylph, proferring the pair of elegant designer sunglasses which he always carries especially for that purpose.

Even with this tragick ending, we all dream of a holiday ROMANCE like the one above. Better two weeks of passion, we think, than none at all. But if other Worriers are remotely like *moi*, then the nearest we will come will be a wet afternoon in Bognor with Kevin Snoad, who treated me to two games in the amusement arcade and half a bag of chips before trying to insist on a quickie behind the pier.

Britain is not a great place for holiday ROMANCE. And whatever the venue, the result is always the same: you write eight long letters and are lucky to get a postcard. If you do, it says: *Hope your OK. Im fine. Met a great new bird in magaluf. Kevin.*

INFATUATION

Is when you get obsessed with somebody, usually someone you have only just glimpsed and never talked to – and you just can't stop thinking about them. Ye film star Brad Pitpony has this effect on *moi*, or did have, as now I am fifteen I have thrown away such childish dreams in order to search for the True Meaning of ROMANCE. However, it is possible to be infatuated with the boy/gurl-next-door or whatever and it can be V. Painful when you linger about hoping to bump into them casually and they pass by as if you were but a flea. They don't do this to be mean but simply because, sadly, they have failed to notice your existence. If they *have* noticed you, because you have taken care to send them ill-disguised Valentines, lurve notes Etck or because you gaze at them with doggy affection whenever they appear, they will probably feel flattered. If you push it, though, they will feel cheesed off. If they are Nasty (sadly, objects of infatuation can be nasty) they may take advantage of you and then reject you. It is better to be infatuated from afar, as real ROMANCE can only happen when both people are involved and really no-one sensible wants to go out with someone who hangs on their every werd and drools as if they were a deity. If anyone did that to you, you'd think they were a few crumbs short of a slice of bread, wouldn't you?

JEALOUSY

The green-eyed monster. Why is it called that? Why *green* with envy? Why not blue? Or red? El Chubb's theory of colour cannot help but make her wonder why the colour of grass, trees and natural planties should be associated with the corkscrewing sense of overpowering dume you feel when yr beLurved walks off with someone much cleverer, prettier, wittier, sportier Etck Etck than you.

However, it is a monster which attacks all of us from time to time (*moi*, most of the time). You feel its fiery tendrils when the object of your affection objects to your affections and flings his arse (sorry, arms) around Tania Melt instead. The worst kind of jealousy though is not when you are wishing you could go out with someone and feeling dead jealous of the people who *are* going out with them – it is the jealousy you feel when you are with someone and think they might be seeing someone else. This is how I have felt on two occasions with Daniel and on one with Adam. I still lie awake nights just wondering who he lurves, now he is in Los Angeles (sigh).

The only ways you can deal with jealousy are:

a) Try not to feel it in the first place. This involves becoming a Buddhist and learning not to want.

3) Standing outside house of beLurved and howling like banshee. This involves unacceptable loss of dignity.

E) Locking self in room and sobbing until someone (probably yr poor old mum) comes to show they care.

F) BUT the most sensible (who ever said Teenage Worriers were sensible?) thing to do would be to realize that if your rival is preferred to you, then you can't be happy with this lurve object in the first place. If they are stupid enough just to like her because she sings like lark, has hair like angel, bazooms of sex goddess Etck then they are not classy enough to appreciate what's specially you, commune meaningfully with yr Soul Etck.

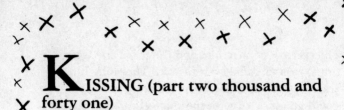

KISSING (part two thousand and forty one)

The reason many Teenage Worriers Worry so much about how to Kiss, is they are scared they will blow the Big Moment of the First Kiss, by producing

A) V. wet slobbery ones that make the recipient feel they have been leapt on by V. friendly, ancient dog

B) V. Dry rasping ones that sandpaper a few layers off beLurved's luscious lips; not opening mouth wide enough so teeth collide, doing untold damage that will mean centuries in the dentist's torture chamber, negotiating complicated co-production with bank, National Lottery Etck

C) Opening mouth too wide and finding it full of beLurved's nose and chin

D) Missing target altogether and ending up with mouthful of leather jacket

E) Being unable to breathe while kissing and therefore emitting noise like drowning rodent OR having to stop at high point in order to breathe in lungfuls of fresh mountain air (unlikely if venue is alley behind dustbins, or *Le Club Tarantulla*).

I've long argued that kissing shld be on National Curriculum. I spot a gap in the Market. If you can't get it on the school curriculum, why not go Private? If you know any V. sinuous sexperienced people, why not suggest they put an ad in their local paper offering sex tuition and kissing lessons to Teenage Worriers? Naturally I am not talking about seedy types who offer ads for demolishing temporary erections, or offering large white chests with no drawers for sale. I am talking about V. Kind people who would TEACH, but not take advantage. Am I an innocent abroad?

But kissing does come naturally with someone you like – it does, *really*, as I have discovered with Adam (moan gnash, tragic demeanour, will I ever feel like that again, Etck). However much I say this, though, you don't believe *moi*, so here, at last, are El

Chubb's definitive kissing tips. **Please read once, then never again**, otherwise you will keep thinking: Have I missed out Stage One? What comes next? Etck. Then the whole point of kissing will be lost . . .

ESSENTIAL KISSING TIPS

<u>KISSING TIP</u> (No.468): Do <u>NOT</u> arrange mouth in kissing position until in close proximity to Lurve object, for fear of dissuading same.

1. Make sure you are warm. A cold nose in the eye and chapped lips do little for passion.
2. Relax. Think hot maple syrup.
3. Trace shape of beLurved's lips with finger.
4. Murmur sweet nothing.
5. Rub your cheek against beLurved's cheek. (Make sure you use face.)

6. If yr beLurved has a wisp of hair floating across
face, take it gently between yr lips and move it to
side (this was a V.Seductive trick of Adam's and I
writhe to think he might be doing this with
Another as I write). But naturally harder with
partner who has Afro or crew cut.

  7. Move lips slowly towards beLurved's. Hover.

  8. Draw back a moment to whisper another sweet
nothing.

  9. Place lips (closed) on beLurved's.

10. Purse lips and move them about. Open them
V. Slightly.

11. Phew. Kiss then continues in variety of ways,
the best of which is that beLurved moves tip of
tongue into yr mouth and your tongue then
connects with your beLurved's. I hope BOYZ are
reading this cos they cld do with a few tips from
Daniel Hope. After which whole business gets
hungry, steamy Etck. I cannot prescribe future
moves cos it takes a minimum of two people to
make a good kiss and you can't be sure what each of
them will do next. What I can say, is if you want to
build up good head of steam, then keep it all
V. SLOW.

  Er, and DON'T do anything you don't want to do
or are not prepared for. A boy f'rinstance who wants
to take it further but has 'forgotten' his condoms is a
boy Not Worth Bothering About. Here endeth first
lesson in kissing. Now put self in ice bucket and
forget about it until you are twenty-one.

LEAP YEAR

This is supposed to be the time when a gurl can propose marriage to a boy, but nowadays I hope liberated Teenage Worriers have no fear of proposing in any year (except normal fear of millstones round neck, life of domestic glume Etck).

LOVE LETTERS

These, like poems, are the most composed and least read of all Teenage Worriers' outpourings. Who among you has not lain awake imagining a letter they will send to their beLurved, only to realize, as the chill dawn stretches its clammy fingers Etck, that you simply don't have the courage. And what about the letters that you get? No-one can write one nearly as good as the one in your imagination . . .

V. sad point of Teenage Worriers' lives in 21st century may be final end of love letter flapping hopefully through letter-box as e.mail dot.com may overtake all handwritten stuff.

However, even if you are all wired up for e.mail, it is good to know how to write a love letter. A few well-chosen werds have V. Powerful effect.

1) Speling it more or less write is going two help. Yore trew luv may think yew stoopid if yew

Embarrassing envelope.

Unspeakably embarrassing envelope. Avoid at all costs.

cant spel. Thiss iz not nessessarilee trew, but a bak-to-baysix noshiun that has cort onn, even amung Teenage wurriers.

2) If you are serious, do not embarrass the recipient by scrawling hearts all over envelope. Also, do not write S.W.A.L.K. (sealed with a loving kiss) or 'Hurry postman don't be slow, this is for my Romeo' on the back. Your true lurve probably has a younger sibling who will tease him or her mercilessly at the sight of such stuff.

3) Say something about the time you last met, that will feel special. Something original, like *I love the way your mouth goes up at the corners even when you aren't smiling*. Or *I never thought an anorak could look OK with dreadlocks, but you've taught me different*, or something.

Lust

Lust is strong fizzical attraction, often confused with 'fancying'. But fancying someone and lusting after them are subtly different, as 'fancying' implies actually liking them a bit whereas 'lust' is more, ahem, rampant. It makes you feel: *cor, phew, sweat, pant, don't-care-what-they're-really-like-just-got-to-have-'em*. If boy approaches you in such a way, yell 'NO' and run. Unless, of course, you feel the same.

Marriage

L. Chubb sez: Teenage Worriers should not get married. Course, if you want to tie knot when V. Old, like 25, then V. nice (wish own parents had got married, might have made me more secure, Etck. Sob).

L. Chubb nose ring. ➔ Put it on yr Lurved one's Hooter and LEAD them around.

Monogamy

Although if you believed the newspapers you would think Teenage Worriers were at it like rabbits with every available passing person, most of us are V.V. ROMANTIC and, when you are ROMANTICally in love, you cannot imagine ever being with anyone else, so monogamy is an essential part of ROMANCE.

Even if I do have more than one love affair I am sure I will turn out to be at the very least a serial monogamist as I can't even talk to more than one boy at once.

Naughty Bits

Victorian times are past – when men swooned with fright when they discovered their wives didn't have willies, or did have pubic hair, or whatever it was – and now we all know better. But DO we? After years of giggling at the mention of bums, willies Etck and making rude noises to annoy grown-ups, deep embarrasment descends during the Teenage Worrier years at the thought of any Naughty Bit being mentioned in front of any adults. If you have reached this stage, you have probably started Worrying about your own Naughty Bits. These

Worries are usually concerned with shape, size, angle, or lack. The overwhelming question is: Are my naughty bits Normal?

The almost certain answer to this question is, yes.

Teenagers lie awake Worrying they might be different from everyone else and have no idea what size or shape their bits shld actually be. Well, kids, you're right. We are *all* different and no willy or vagina is exactly the same, so there. Sexual development also starts at very different times so there's no point in a thirteen-year-old gurl or boy even thinking about how small their willy or bazooms are until they are five years older. That's just the way it is. Not that it stops me Worrying about my miniscule bazooms, but at least it helps to know others are in the same *bâteau*.

The point, ahem, of Naughty Bits in ROMANTIC terms, is that they are Focal Points (that werd again) for seething pashiones Etck. This is why it is a V.Good idea to keep them under wraps if you are keen not to go too far. Don't ever make the mistake of thinking your bazooms are so small that no-one will like them. Or too big, either.

I would like to start a fashion for a new naughty bit. I would choose the earlobe, since earlobes are V. sensitive to nibbling Etck and could become just as naughty, with a little encouragement, as the bazoom. Also, they are freely available to both sexes. Ear lobe covers would be a must, in a variety of gorgeous fabrics and colourways – appliquéd, sequinned, whatever. Then, on hot summer days, we could all walk around naked except for our lobe covers. This would cheer up everyone who is Worried about their current naughty bits, cos no-one would pay any attention to willies or bazooms any more and all attention would be focused on the LOBE.

As all imaginative Teenage Worriers will have noted, those with tiny lobes, or lugs like taxi doors, would suffer.

No

V. Imp accessory for the ROMANTICally inclined, as a 'no' said early will prevent all kinds of future heartbreak.

A famous myth is that '*No doesn't always mean no.*' Oh, yes it does.

There will always be a few tragic boyz who think that, while a gurl knows what 'yes' and 'no' mean in everyday English, she means something completely different if she's talking about sex. If a gurl says no, and a boy forces her to have sex, this is rape. No-one ever ever *ever* has to have sex unless they want to. Don't *ever* feel guilty for saying no.

And, if someone says 'no' to you, just accept it. You can always try again later, to see if they've changed their mind.

El Chubb's TIP: practise chatting up boyz from age of twelve. Try it espesh on the V. handsome, world-weary ones who are bound to say *Non* and then you will not weep and moan and pull your hairs out one by one in anguish if Turned Down later when you really mean it, as you will be quite used to handling it.

NB Have plan ready if someone you don't like accepts and thinks this means they can have their wicked way with you. eg: 'I was only practising', 'I thought you were somebody else', 'I thought I was somebody else', Etck Etck.

ORGASM

Also known as 'coming' (and sadly, often a prelude to boy going), this is the big bit of overwhelming Feeling (surge, throb, choirs of birdies, clash of cymbals, raging waterfalls Etck) you get at the

culmination of ye sexual act, or while doing things
to your own Naughty Bits. Some V. Romantic
people think you can get an orgasm just by looking
at the one you feel V. ROMANTIC about, but even
I, with all my seething pashiones, flowing juices
Etck, find this hard to believe.

PHEROMONES

Obviously, these little chemical attractants have
been working on the human race for centuries,
without our even knowing it. They doubtless made
the pharoahs moan, too, and perhaps that's how they
got their name.

PORNOGRAPHY

*Pheromones
(or fleas?)*

This is a word that sends parents running
screaming. The idea that their offspring might have
rude pictures of gurlz or boyz stuffed under their
pillow is too much for them. BUT, although there is
horrible pornography, there is also a lot of stuff that
most boyz are bound to look at some time or
another – and it seems to be catching on for gurlz
too.

*See Naughty Pix
on next Page →.
(if you move FAST)*

The main prob with these pix is they don't look like many real gurlz, ie: they have vast bazooms, curves where most of us have dents, and dents where most of us have big fat roly bits. The gurlz who pose for them often got their bits from a plastic sturgeon (sorry, surgeon) and I find it V. Tragick waste of human potential that this is all they can think to do with their life.

And then she RIPPED the flimsy covering to reveal, a LONG, FIRM, GLISTENING bar of fudge

Whatever turns you on...

One thing you can say about any kind of porn is that it's definitely not ROMANTIC.

62

PREGNANCY

> **PREGNANT?** But I thought you were on the **pill**...

> I **WAS** on the pill, but every time we **DO IT** I roll off...

The scene is a candlelit fast-food joint. A beautiful Teenage Worrier is stirring her milkshake, with a wistful, dreamy, faraway look in her soulful eyes. There are no burgers because of the power cut. It is freezing cold. But she is warmed by a secret knowledge. She can't wait to tell Clint Cleft, the Love-of-her-life, the marvellous news. The door opens and an icy blast from the freezing mean streets of the throbbing urban jungle blows in. And so does Clint Cleft. They have known each other for six whole months and now she knows that soon they will be as ONE. Clint approaches, his boyish smile decorating his manly chops, his long limbs purposeful, blah blah . . .

Gurl: Darling, I've got some wonderful news.

Clint: Oh good. I'm glad you're happy, because there's something I want to tell you, too.

Gurl: Don't you want to know what it is?

Clint: No, that's fine, as long as you're pleased, because . . .

Gurl: There are no longer two of us in this relationship, sweetheart, there are three.

Clint: But I know. That's what I was going to tell you. I'm SO pleased you don't mind.

Gurl: How did you know? I've only just found out myself. And why should I mind?

Clint: Well, you know, I thought you'd be jealous.

Gurl: Jealous? Of our little baby?

Clint: Well, I wouldn't exactly call Gloria Scroggins a *baby* – I mean, she's got whopping . . .

Gurl: Gloria Scroggins! What's Gloria Scroggins got to do with it?

Clint: But you just said you *knew*. I've been seeing her for about a month . . .

Gurl: Boooo hoooo. Sob. Monster. Etck.

This tragic scenario is played up and down the country every day. So is another, involving the dreadful panic of late periods, over-the-counter pregnancy tests, huge relief, huger despair. Those ads that say a puppy is not just for Christmas, but for life, would be better applied to babies, since around 100,000 Teenagers a year become pregnant

64

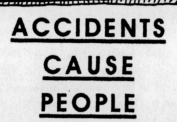

ACCIDENTS
CAUSE
PEOPLE

and most of these are unplanned. It really is the most important thing of all to check out and use contraception before you get near sex, because by the time you are near, you may find yourself actually Doing It and then it will be Too Late. Arg, squirm, cling to virginity as to life-belt in raging ocean Etck.

PRUDERY

Is when people are V. Disapproving of sex and do not like to admit it is taking place. When the Victorians covered piano-legs in lace knickers, it was a sign of prudery. Although if they thought Men wld get excited and mount the piano, maybe they had a rather exaggerated view of the carnal instinct after all. Prudery usually leads to hypocrisy and people turning blind eyes, telling fibs Etck to keep harmony. Alternatively, it can just be a sign that sex is not your cup of tea and that your cup of tea is more likely to be – a cup of tea. Why not?

QUESTIONS

ROMANTIC QUESTIONS: EL CHUBB'S LIST
Write the numbers 1,2,3,4 in any order several times, on piece of paper. This is yr special personal chart. Choose a question and then close your eyes and wave your finger around before stabbing it down on chart. Then look up answer, ie: if you score a 2 for question B, you look up B2.
A)   Does the object of my desire lurve me?
B)   Does the one I am thinking of think of me as much as I think of them?
C)   Is the thing that I dread going to happen?

66

D) Has he/she done it as many times as they say?

E) Will I be a virgin for long?

F) Will my nose/bazooms/willy get any bigger?

Answers

a1) Yes a2) Much more than you think a3) More than you love them a4) Why? Do you lurve them?

B1) Far more B2) Nearly B3) Depends what you mean by 'think' B4) Ask them

C1) Never C2) Depends how good your contraception was C3) Nothing as bad as you dread will happen C4) No

D1) More D2) No, they haven't done it at all D3) Not quite D4) Exactly

E1) As long as you choose E2) Ages E3) Six years, ten months, one week, four days and two hours E4) No

F1) No, smaller F2) Yes, much F3) So big you'll need to get doors specially widened if you go in sideways F4) Exactly the right size

Tips for analysing oracle

If you believe a single word of any of the above replies, you are V. Gullible. How could *moi* possibly know anything about you? F'rinstance, how could the answers: E3) or F3) possibly be true? The same is obviously true of all the other answers only, like those daft quizzes in magazines like *Smirk* and *Yoo Hoo*, they are more cleverly disguised and give the appearance of TRUTH: beware quizzes, gentle reader.

Red roses

Still best ROMANTIC gift. Cheapest, too, if you have any growing, since flowers from own garden or windowbox still most ROMANTIC of all. Do not, however, confuse geraniums with roses; geraniums do not pick well.

Answer to question on page 37

A: V. sorry, but can't remember whether ALL of the boyz are gay, or NONE of them. Never mind, eh?

Seasons

Winter: What cld be more ROMANTIC than a snowy stroll, mufflers entwined, throwing crumbs to swans as they glide along icy lakeside? Even the scarlet nose of yr companion, complete with frozen drip, cannot detract from Winter's paradise . . .

Spring: is ye traditional season for ROMANCE. What cld be more ROMANTIC than a Spring stroll, patting the curly heads of bouncy lambs who bleat their cheerful bleats as they Spring through cowslips, primroses Etck? Even as you slip on cowpats, you may clutch the hand of your belurved...

Summer: nothing, surely, cld be more ROMANTIC than a hot, hazy, stroll along a golden beach, entwined in the strong arms of . . . Etck. (But see HOLIDAY ROMANCES for, um, downside.)

Autumn: season of mists and mellow nostalgia much belurved of teenage Worriers. What cld be more ROMANTIC than wandering through crackling leaves, the smell of bonfires in your hooter? So what if you are wandering alone; the season itself will instill you with all the same feeling you get with ROMANCE: melancholy, longing, yearning, shivering, unspeakable glume Etck, Etck.

The Romance

Ah! Ye Romance of WINTER: Season of Red roses,
I mean, noses.

Bless the Sexy SPRING, as it brings Hay Fever.

of the Seasons

The sultry SUMMER: season of SWEAT.

Turn over a new leaf and FALL for someone in Autumn.

SEX

Steam COR phew
SHEAT

When middle-aged Worriers think about their own
dear little Teenage Worriers having sex, they
tremble with trepidation. This is because middle-
aged Worriers remember their own mis-spent yoof
and although they wish they had mis-spent a bit
more of it they are scared their own offspring will be
Doing It all the time and fail their exams, have
babies, get STDs (sexually transmitted diseases)
Etck, Etck. What many of them have forgotten is
how Worried they were about Sex themselves and
how little of it they actually did. This is still true of
Teenage Worriers today. Apparently the average age
for first having sex is seventeen. Since people always
lie about such things, this is quite likely to make
the average age older. Also it could mean that even
those who are Doing It at seventeen have only done
it once. Even if all seventeen-year-olds did it several
times a week (V.V. Unlikely, where would they
go?), it still means that loads of other people have
sex for the first time much later (and that doesn't
count all the people who never have it at all . . .).

ROMANCE is V. Obvious prelude to SEX, but
there doesn't have to be much sex at all in a
ROMANCE, which can be a meeting of minds, or a
brushing of fingertips, and still take up a bigger
proportion of your heart, mind, head Etck than

outrageous nooky with someone you're not that interested in as a person. There's lots of pressure to get off with people as a Teenage Worrier. You don't have to. Wait till you really like someone. In my case, sadly, the people I really like always get off with someone else, sob. But perhaps one day . . . yearn.

Kissing, cuddling and canoodling are all part of sex and you are having a sexual relationship if you are doing any of these – *and* it's much safer than full intercourse.

Meanwhile, here are El Chubb's answers to just some of the Sex Worries y'all have sent moi:

DON'T CONDOMS WRECK ROMANCE?
Opposite, obviously is true. STDs, pregnancies and endless Worry Etck wreck it, seriously. I have been carrying a pack of three condoms around ever since I can remember, but sadly I have never had the chance to offer them to my beLurved in moment of high pashione. (Must check their sell-by date.)

HE/SHE SEZ THEY WON'T GO OUT WITH ME UNLESS I DO IT. SO SHOULD I?
Pressure is not Romance. Your reply: get lost, sucker, plenty more fish in ocean Etck. (NB, although yr personal ocean may currently seem polluted and fish-free, you still have to think this way. Another bus *will* come along eventually.)

73

*I'M SCARED IT MIGHT HURT AND THERE'LL
BE LOADS OF BLOOD.*
V.V.V.V. Unlikely. See also VIRGINITY.

*WILL HE/SHE THINK LESS OF ME IF WE DO
IT?*
It has been known for a gurl to sleep with her
dreamboat only to hear that dreaded werd *'slag'*. If
such a boy is your dreamboat, could be you need a
brain transplant. Check him OUT, then chuck him
out.

IF WE HAVE SEX, WILL EVERYONE KNOW?
No. Having sex does not cause your Bits to glow in
the dark, or change your fizzical appearance in any
way. So unless you or your partner spray-paint the
lavvies or tattoo your foreheads with the message
'We've dunnit', no-one will know. An element of
mutual trust is obviously useful.

*IF SOMEONE SEEMS TO HAVE DONE IT WITH
LOTS OF PEOPLE, SURELY THAT MEANS
THEY'LL DO IT WITH ME?*
Arggg. Are any of you this stoopid? You know
YOU wouldn't just do it with anyone, so why
should someone else? And would you WANT to do
it with someone who does it with everyone?

WORRY WORRY WORRY WORRY

74

I'M 22 AND I HAVEN'T DONE IT. DOES THIS MEAN I'M A WIMP?

This wd usually be a question asked by a boy, since gurlz who do it later are, unfairly, never called wimps, but put on pedestals Etck. Yawn. But boyz, as well as gurlz, should wait till they're ready to do it with someone they really like. Such a boy wld get more respeck from *moi*, I know that (gnash, moan, is Adam doing it with Another?).

Sofa

Yes! If you do not have a trew lurve with whom to be ROMANTIC, a sofa is a great replacement. Sofas are warm and cuddly, let you lie full length on them whenever you want without complaining and never disagree with a word you say. (Once you do get a ROMANCE going, introduce him or her to your sofa as soon as possible, har har leer.)

TELEPHONE

My Adored Father's inability to pay a telephone bill on time means that for about half the year our phone is cut off. This is a tragick disadvantage when it comes to ROMANCE. Just when I am longing to whisper melting sweet nothings into eager receiver Etck, there is nothing sweet but whirr and cackle of static. However, the fact that siblings, parents Etck are picking up telephone extensions to eavesdrop or blow raspberries means that most ROMANTIC telephone conversations are more likely to go like this:

Brrrrrrrr Brrrrrrrr

Teenage Worrier 1: Hi

Teenage Worrier 2: Hi

Teenage Worrier 1: It's me

Teenage Worrier 2: U-huh

Teenage Worrier 1: How you doing?

Teenage Worrier 2: Fine.

Teenage Worrier 1: Great.

Teenage Worrier 2: You OK?

Teenage Worrier 1: Fine.

Teenage Worrier 2: Great.

Teenage Worrier 1: yeh

Teenage Worrier 2: Well, uh, see you around

Teenage Worrier 1: yeh

Teenage Worrier 2: bye

Teenage Worrier 1: yeh

The above is a direct transcript of a Teenage Worrier's long-awaited phone call. What she went on to do immediately afterwards, was to phone three frendz in turn and discuss each element of above, ie: what did 'uh-huh' mean in the context of the conversation? How was she to interpret 'great'? The best bit, all the frendz agreed, was 'see you around' which gave great cause for hope. The fact that the BOY had phoned at all was also V. Exciting, everyone thought. Arg. Maybe it is better to have phone on blink than to be forced to endure such tortures.

TRUST

When you decide, in heat of pashione, to allow that lingering kiss to go a little further, only to find that your bra size is pinned on the school noticeboard the following day, you can bet your life your Trust has been Betrayed. Avoiding such humiliations means only snogging V. Nice trustworthy people who you like and who like you. Your intuition shld tell you who they are. NB When drunk, or under influence of other intoxicating substances, intuition is V.Blunt.

Underwear

As ROMANCE progresses (sigh), the chances are that underwear may become visible. You do not have to be at the stage of actually removing it to start Worrying about it. In fact, I have been Worrying about my own underwear since I was six years old and realized I had to display it to the whole class in PE lessons. Oh woe, those holes . . . those mortifying colour combinations. My little brother Benjy still suffers same indignity if my Only Mother forces him to wear pants with pictures of Timmy the tractor on . . .

Ye Boxer shorts are beating up Y-Fronts in battle
for boyz underbits.

However, if you're addicted to *Smirk*, you will be
bombarded by styles and materials. Arg. F'rinstance,
in a recent issue of *Yoo Hoo*, we could choose from
white lycra cotton vest and shorts, white lacey
v-neck T-shirt and shorts . . . silver satin vest and
brief set . . . white ribbed T-shirt with meshed
flowers (*what!*) or a blue velour T-shirt and white
heart knickers. Arg. The cheapest of these little
outfits is more than yours truly will ever see in a
month. Stay cheap and simple with . . . *Letty
Chubb's Underwear Tips*:

Keep it clean.

Keep it neat.

Keep it snowy white or sooty black.

The tragedy of the pale grey knicker that should
have been dazzlingly white can be avoided by
buying black, but black too, can turn to fog. But

wait! Is this El Chubb enslaving herself and other Teenage Worriers in the heartrending pit of *looksism*? How can a plain grey knicker be a *tragedy*? Get Real. Who cares if your knickers are beige or grey? Up with mushroom panties! Down with white panties! (whooops). Fact is, nice, neat, non-baggy underwear is appealing on both sexes so, um, I think I'll stick with convention on this one. No need for fabu-bras (nothing to put in them in the sad case of *moi*, anyway) or negligees in floaty wisps. Just clean white bits to cover your bits. Same goes for boyz and gurlz, OK? NB Boyz, no boxer shorts with naked women on them (pictures, I mean), per-leeze.

VALENTINES

It is V. Cruel the way, year after year, Feb 14th comes round just after Feb 13th (not that I believe 13 is unlucky, but Feb 13th does make you V. Nervy and glumey) and yet it never EVER brings a Valentine from the person you're hoping to hear from. There may well be well-meaning Valentines from your aunty or little brother or even one, in my case, from Brian Bolt . . . but I know this year I will look in vain for a Los Angeles postmark . . .

I have even got my reply card ready. On the front it says: *What?? Be YOUR Valentine? You lousy no-good two-timer! And on the inside, it says: Of course . . .* But I feel it is destined to stay in my bedside table along with the other Valentines I have bought over the years and never sent. Sob, self-pity Etck.

L. CHUBB'S TIP TO CHEER UP VALENTINES DAY

Lonely Hearts Party
Ask everyone who hasn't got a boy/gurlfriend to come. Put on V.V. sad music, or a tape of rain pattering into puddles, or sound effects of wailing violins or banshees. All stand in a circle and sob loudly. Who knows? Maybe a kindly tissue will be offered to you by an intriguing stranger . . . Think how V. ROMANTIC yr meeting will seem many years from now when you are old and grey.

NB When aroused by lust and indeed by ROMANCE, the human heart beats faster. I guess this is why it is used for valentines and all other symbols of lurve. But it doesn't change half as much as the male willy does when aroused (so I am told, ahem) so why not put Big Willies on Valentine's Cards Etck? Another thing that happens is you sweat more. How about lovely big fat drops of SWEAT?

   CAMPAIGN for sweaty Valentines!

VESTS

string vest (Nice)

L. Chubb Best vest gone west

Not most ROMANTIC of accessories (see
UNDERWEAR, earlier) but useful if you still can't
really fill a bra (sob, cringe) and don't want to reveal
whole bod during canoodling.

VIRGINS

Rather comforting to think that everyone has been
one of these and most Teenage Worriers, *moi*self
included, still are. I'm beginning to think it would
be nice just to Do It once, then not bother about it
again, as the Worry involved gives me sleepless
nights.

In ye olden daze it was V. Imp to be a virgin
when you married, if you were a gurl. This was so
the man wld be sure any offspring of the union were
his alone (though what stopped you from Doing It
with someone else in the afternoons I have no idea).
People were so keen to prove they were virgins that
they even had little fake bags of blood so they could
pretend their hymen (the wafer-thin covering across
the vagina) had broken on Day One of the
honeymoon. In fact, now as then, most gurlz'
hymens are broken long before they have sex, either
just by running about, or riding a bike, or anything,

NO

VIRGINS Я US

CHASED, BUT CHASTE

Hi Men I'm Keeping my Hymen

Celibate and PROUD

SLOW DOWN Legs crossing

and they don't even notice it. So the fear of agony, tearing and pouring bludde on your first sexshual encounter is one more Worry crossed off list (phew).

I am a grate believer, despite aforesaid worry about being a virgin, in having a ROMANTIC time the first time. It seems a bit glumey to think of a quickie behind the dustbins like poor old Rover, or a feverish snog while babysitting on a neighbour's sofa that goes too far – especially if the neighbours return in the middle and wonder why you are upside down with a hunk instead of glueing your ear to the baby alarm as you shld be . . .

For *moi*, it will be in a waterbed with Adam Stone – or Nothing (Pretty easy to guess which . . .). I s'pose I'll end up V. Proud of my virginity when I'm an old lady of thirty. In fact, I am determined to be V. Proud of it Now.

WATER

Ye ROMANCE of water! What cld be more ROMANTIC than a stroll by a moonlit lake? Or splashing in a cule pule on Californian mountainside? Or sitting by fountain (cor, spurt, Etck) in a sunny pizza, I mean piazza, listening to gentle strumming of stomach juices accompanied by gurgling of guitar?

There is an old psychology trick that asks you to think of some kind of water. Go on, do it now.

85

What did you think of?

Ocean means you are V. Sexy.

Sea, ditto but less.

Lake, calmly sensual.

Stream, working on it.

I always think of a dripping tap, which goes to prove such Deep Insights into Yuman condition are V. Unsound.

Let's hear it for WATER! Biggest ROMANTIC ingredient of all! (Also, if you drink same, less likely to end up in V. UnROMANTIC situation leading to regret, pining Etck.)

X CITEMENT

(OK, excitement, but I'm not doing XYLOPHONES in ROMANCE, and I've done KISSING, so there.)

What is ROMANCE without that fluttering of the heart, panting of the, er, pants, trembling of the nether regions (must check what a nether is before handing in buke) that accompanies a first date . . . or kiss. The excitement of seeing someone you really like the look of and (gulp) finding that they like the look of you too. Having checked it actually is you they're talking to (in the case of *moi*, it's usually Hazel, who is standing behind me, that has caused their eyes to light up and their willies, I mean spirits, to rise) you are now in a position to offer them your phone number. Excitement!

ROMANCE!

The next step is sitting by the phone. It rings! Excitement!

ROMANCE!

It is for your mum. It rings again. Excitement!

ROMANCE!

It is for your dad! It rings again. Excitement!

ROMANCE!

It is your beLurved. Double Excitement!

Double ROMANCE!

Then you get all that stuff about where to meet. Then there's the ten hours of getting ready, by which time the excitement is at such a fever pitch that no-one on earth could live up to your expectations. Never mind. Excitement is what ROMANCE is all about . . .

... which leads us to ...

Yes

(ok, if you like, yeah, yup, u-huh, mmm).

This may be the moment when you cast cares to the wind and decide to wallow in undiluted pashione. But it may equally be the time when you want to say Yes to a kiss, Yes to canoodling, but No to anything else. If ROMANCE is blossoming, this will not deter your lurve object (see SEX, earlier). And together you can waft on a sea of ROMANCE, saying Yes to all the things you both like, and even some of the things you're not crazy about but know your lurved one likes (by this, I mean consenting to watch mud-wrestling, not hanging upside down in frogman's flippers and beating yourself with a wet haddock).

However true my ROMANCE is, I will never however say Yes to fish and chips (can't stand fish).

Zits

If a lonely zit is wandering the universe, searching for a home, it will zero in on Brian's sizeable conk even before my own. Yet even Adam has zits. And I lurve every last spot of them. So you see, although they plague the Teenage Worrier who has them, ROMANCE *can* shine through.

88

ENDPIECE

And now, dear reader, we end our brief stroll through the vineyards of ROMANCE. With sinking hearts, we bid farewell to the groves of grapes, eternal sunshine, sifting sands, twinkling fountains, scarlet blooms, golden summers Etck of our imagination and turn our sinking hearts once more to Sluggs Comprehensive, GCSEs, and our best chance of ROMANCE — a clash of teeth, or braces, with Syd Snogg round the corner.

And we ask ourselves: does ROMANCE really exist?

My answer, dearest reader, is yes, briefly, only to end in tears in the tragick case of moi . . . and yet, Hope does spring eternal, and even now, El Chubb is dusting herself off, writing one last heartfelt epistle to Adam Stone before brushing wig for first time in months and facing werld with Spring in Step.

Who knows who might be waiting round next corner? What sweet nothings he might murmur? True ROMANCE can lie in smallest places, in cosiest corners, in a look, in a werd . . . and we all may find it someday . . .

Yrs truly,

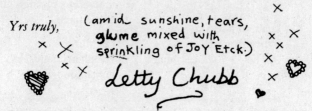

(amid sunshine, tears, glume mixed with sprinkling of JOY Etck.)

Letty Chubb

Help!

Useful telephone numbers

CONTRACEPTION

Brook Advisory Centres
0171 713 9000 (helpline, office hours)
0171 617 8000 (recorded information helpline)
Contraceptive and counselling service for the under 25s. Local clinics throughout the UK. Under 16s can obtain confidential help.

Family Planning Association
0171 837 5432 (confidential helpline)
Clinics throughout the UK. Can also send V. helpful leaflets.

GAY/LESBIAN

Lesbian and Gay Switchboard
0171 837 7324 (24 hours, Mon to Fri)

Advice and info service that also offers advice for friends and family. NB They are really hard to get through to, but don't give up.

North London Lesbian and Gay Project
0171 607 8346
Run the lesbian, gay and bisexual Youth Project for under 25s, and can provide advice, info and education resources.

PROBLEMS

Youth Access
0181 772 9900
Details of young people's counsellors throughout the country.

Childline
~~Free~~phone 0800 1111
For children only.